Original title:
The Charm of the Day

Copyright © 2025 Creative Arts Management OÜ
All rights reserved.

Author: Elias Marchant
ISBN HARDBACK: 978-1-80586-138-6
ISBN PAPERBACK: 978-1-80586-610-7

## Sunny Shenanigans

Morning sun looks sly and bright,
Birds are chirping, what a sight!
Coffee spills on my new shirt,
Laughter echoes, life's a flirt.

Squirrels steal my afternoon snack,
Chasing them, I trip, oh crack!
A dog barks loud, gives me a scare,
Chasing tails, we're in midair.

Clouds parade, so fluffy, grand,
They look like pillows, soft and planned.
I pretend to nap on the grass,
But ants decide to join, alas!

Evening comes with goofy sights,
Dancing shadows, silly lights.
Daylight fades, but fun won't cease,
Tomorrow brings more joy and peace.

## Moments Wrapped in Sunshine

Socks mismatched, and hats askew,
Laughter dances in sunshine's hue.
A dog steals sandwiches, oh what a sight,
Picnic chaos brings pure delight.

Chasing squirrels in a frantic race,
Everyone trips, a comical chase.
Cakes with frosting, they're quite a mess,
Sweet sticky fingers, happiness to confess.

## The Gift of a Starlit Evening

Stars all twinkle, wearing their best,
Carrying wishes from east to west.
Someone trips over a dozen chairs,
As laughter erupts, floating in the airs.

Crickets play music, quite off-key,
While fireflies flicker, shining with glee.
S'mores ignite, a gooey delight,
Chocolate fingers — a hilarious sight.

## Breezes that Kiss the Skin

Gentle winds whisper, tickle your nose,
Blowing hats off, where did it go?
Chasing a paper boat down the stream,
Joining the laughter, living the dream.

Sunshine slides in with a silly grin,
While lemonade spills, oh where to begin?
Swings make us fly, feet touch the sky,
A flip and a flap, and oh, my, oh my!

## Soliloquy of the Brilliant Horizon

Sunset paints colors that scream and shout,
While seagulls cackle, they flaunt about.
A tumble, a roll, in the sandy gold,
Grains in our pockets, laughter untold.

Flip-flops and footprints, a joyful scene,
As waves crash down, in a comic routine.
The day's wild tales, they wrap us tight,
With chuckles and giggles that last through the night.

## **Echoes of a Bright Awakening**

The rooster crows, a quirky sound,
Running late, my socks not found.
I trip on shoes, a bumpy ride,
With giggles now, I take this stride.

The coffee spills, a darkened spot,
My dog just stole a donut, hot!
Chasing him 'round the kitchen floor,
We laugh so hard, we nearly soar.

## Radiance in a Gentle Breeze

The breeze comes in with playful tease,
My hat takes flight, it sails with ease.
A squirrel throws acorns, oh what fun,
We both run fast, who'll be outdone?

The sunbeam dances, cheeky and bright,
Tickling my nose, a joyful sight.
With ants in line, a silly parade,
I stop and stare, my worries fade.

## Lullabies of the Rising Sun

The sun peeks up, a goofy grin,
Waking the world, let games begin!
A cowlick sprouts, my hair's a mess,
Yet laughter wins, I must confess.

Breakfast calls, with eggs that jump,
While jelly slides, a tasty lump.
I slip and slide, a syrupy fate,
In this wild morn, who could relate?

## **Glimmers of Hope at Midday**

Midday sun, a glowing orb,
I try to read, my thoughts absorb.
A fly buzzes, makes my head spin,
With silly swats, I try to win.

Picnic plans under an oak tree,
The ants declare a feast for free!
We laugh and shout, a jolly group,
As lemonade spills, we all regroup.

## Dawn's Gentle Embrace

The rooster crows, what a surprise,
Dreams are lost in morning's rise.
Socks mismatched in a sleepy haze,
Coffee spills in comical ways.

The sun peeks through, a cheeky grin,
Chasing away the night's sly kin.
Cats and kids merge in a race,
To see who claims the sunlit space.

## A Dance with Time

Tick tock goes the clock, so bold,
Yet my breakfast is still cold.
Time does a jig in a wily show,
While I chase it, moving slow.

Laughter rings as slippers fail,
Tripping over socks, now that's a tale.
A two-step with the postman's dog,
We dance around the morning fog.

## **Golden Hour Reverie**

Evening brings a melting light,
Laughter dances, pure delight.
Chasing shadows, we clown around,
Tripping on joy, pure bliss is found.

As dusk wraps us in a cozy hug,
Sudden storms send every bug.
Hats fly off, we all take flight,
Laughter echoes in the fading light.

## The Magic in Mundanity

Monday blues, what a way to start,
Yet socks in the dryer play their part.
Spilled cereal—an artful scene,
Breakfast cuisine—or so it seems.

The garden gnome gives a wink,
As laughter bubbles, we all think.
Life's simple quirks, a daily play,
Finding joy in the ordinary way.

## Revelations in Daylight's Embrace

Waking up, my socks don't match,
The sun sneers through a window catch.
Coffee spills like morning zest,
A cat steals my breakfast, no jest!

Birds chirp loudly, a raucous choir,
While I fumble with laundry fire.
The day unfolds with goofy twists,
Moments like these, how could I resist?

Lawnmowers buzz, a symphony sweet,
Rabbits dance, tapping their feet.
A squirrel stares, he's plotting schemes,
Perhaps my sandwich in his dreams?

As daylight shines on silly claims,
I laugh at life's absurd little games.
For every slip, trip, and misplay,
There's joy tucked neatly in the fray.

**Unwritten Stories Beneath the Sky**

Under blue skies, dandelions sway,
Kids on bikes zoom without delay.
Ice cream drips on a sunny lap,
Alligators chase me? Just a nap!

Sidewalk chalk draws worlds so wild,
Crayons in hand, I feel like a child.
Clouds morph into shapes I can't guess,
Is that a dragon? Or just a mess?

A dog runs by in goofy glee,
Chasing its tail like it's the key.
I wave hello to passing friends,
Sharing jokes as laughter blends.

Underneath the vast, bright dome,
I gather tales, stories roam.
Each moment's a gift, shocking and bright,
In this lively theater of daylight.

## Colors of Bliss at Sunset

As the sun dips low, colors collide,
Purple and orange, a wild ride.
My humor's sparked with each new hue,
Are those flamingos in my view?

Pinks and golds in a playful fight,
A cat sprawls wide, soaking up light.
Mysterious shadows start to sway,
Is it a dance, or just cliché?

The crickets chirp their silly tunes,
While I dodge fireflies and raccoons.
A picnic blanket, full of crumbs,
Who knew sunset could lead to drums?

In evening's glow, we share our cheer,
With tales that tickle and stories dear.
Colors of bliss, laughter to spread,
Goodnight to the day, dreams ahead!

## Glimmers of Magic in Each Hour

Tick-tock, the clock wears a grin,
Time's silly games, where do we begin?
Each tick is a laugh, a dance, a hug,
Coffee's still brewing, oh such a mug!

At noon the puns get thicker, it's true,
My lunchbox sings a song or two.
Hotdogs argue, "We're the main dish!"
While donuts wobble, "We grant each wish!"

A walking stick bug thinks he's a star,
Sashaying past my picnic jar.
Each hour holds magic, rich and bright,
Chasing the shadows, absorbing the light.

As evening nears, the giggles blend,
With heartfelt stories and laughter's trend.
In every tick, a treasure unfolds,
Life's quirky moments, a joy to behold!

## A Warm Embrace from the Sun

The sun rises up, a bright ball of cheer,
It tickles my face, saying, "Come here!"
Birds chirp their tunes, a comedic delight,
As squirrels play tag, oh what a sight!

Laughter erupts from the flowers so bold,
They gossip in colors, stories retold.
Dancing with bees, so clumsy and sweet,
The day makes me grin, I can't feel my feet!

A cloud passes by, it trips on a beam,
It tumbles and puffs like a whipped cream dream.
Sunshine on skin, an outrageous affair,
I bask in this glow, with laughter to spare!

The hourglass winks, its sand takes a dive,
Time plays a trick, making me feel alive.
With sunshine and giggles, my heart skips a beat,
A warm embrace, oh, life's such a treat!

## Strands of Time Spun in Gold

Each moment weaves laughter like fabric of fun,
With threads made of sunshine, oh how they run!
Tick-tock goes the clock, with a mischievous grin,
As I chase after seconds, trying to win.

The wind whispers jokes as it zips through the trees,
It nudges the flowers, making them sneeze!
Time's got a twinkle, a wink in its eye,
As hours pirouette, soaring so high.

A squirrel flips pancakes while singing a tune,
The sky looks bemused, it turns slightly maroon.
Moments keep spinning, like tops in a race,
I laugh with the sunset, a good-natured face!

In this yarn of existence, we're all sewn together,
Each joke shared in time, is light as a feather.
So let's revel in laughter, let our spirits unfold,
For life is a tapestry spun bright with gold!

## **Echoes of Poetry in the Wilderness**

In the woods where the acorns wear tiny hats,
The animals gather, with their witty spats.
A frog croaks a verse, in a voice oh so grand,
While the crickets compose, with their tiny band!

The trees sway and giggle, their branches in play,
As bees form a chorus, in the light of the day.
Squirrels write sonnets on leaves fluttering by,
While owls hoot puns, as they soar through the sky.

A fox dons a scarf, with style so unique,
He struts through the brush, all happy and sleek.
The wind carries laughter, a joyful refrain,
As echoes of poetry dance through the grain.

With humor like petals, the flowers are bold,
Their colors proclaiming stories untold.
In this merry wilderness, where jesters reside,
Laughter is endless, like the moon's cheeky glide!

## The Dance of Time Across the Sky

Twilight tiptoes in, on starry little feet,
As laughter spills softly from night's cozy seat.
The moon starts to giggle, with stars in a spin,
While shadows play tag, letting mischief begin.

Clouds twirl like dancers, all puffy and white,
They tease the horizon, in a playful flight.
Time skips on its toes, with a chuckle and flip,
As evening unfolds, in a bright, silly quip.

With crickets composing their evening ballet,
The world bursts with whimsy, come join in the play!
The day takes a bow, in a spectacle grand,
As night brings its giggles, like magic so planned.

So let's whirl with the moments, in laughter we stand,
With time as our partner, a whimsical band.
We dance under stars, in joy's sweet embrace,
For life's one big jest, as we run this sweet race!

## Whispers of Morning Light

Socks mismatched, what a sight,
Coffee spills in the morning light,
Toast dances like it's gone mad,
Laughter echoes, life isn't bad.

Chickens cluck a gossip spree,
The cat naps on the old TV,
Sunbeams tickle the garden's face,
While we race at a snail's pace.

Pancakes flip in a silly way,
Each one lands in early play,
Butter melts like a soft smile,
Joy unfolds in quirky style.

Morning mischief, chaos and cheer,
Every day brings something dear,
Life's a jest, a grand parade,
In sunshine's glow, our fun displayed.

## **Enchanted Hours**

Tickling breezes, the trees do sway,
A squirrel steals my sandwich away,
Time ambles with a silly dance,
Reminding us to take a chance.

Under the sun, we shout and play,
Making cloud shapes, drifting away,
Giggles echo where shadows blend,
With joyous hearts that never bend.

A garden gnome wearing shades,
Sprinkled fun in sunlight cascades,
While bees buzz in a comic rush,
Nature joins in for a light fuss.

With laughter filling the warm midday,
Life's antics won't drift away,
Each moment's a gift, wild and free,
In the enchanted hours, you'll see.

**Sunlit Serenade**

The sun winks from a golden throne,
While I dance in my flip-flop zone,
A bee tries to steal my drink in jest,
Nature's party, it's quite the fest.

Birds croon silly songs of delight,
Chirping out every wrong note in sight,
With each flub, we cater to cheer,
A melody crafted with laughter near.

Picnics spill forth with snacks galore,
As ants plot a delightful score,
We swat them away with a hearty laugh,
In the sunlit glow, we share our path.

Moments of bliss and quirky glee,
Life's serenade invites you to be,
Joyful tunes fill the open air,
In this sunny scene, without a care.

## **Melody of Everyday Moments**

The toaster plays a familiar tune,
While socks argue on which should swoon,
The clock ticks loud, a playful tease,
In our daily dance, we aim to please.

Sidewalks hum with a buzzing cheer,
As dogs chase tails, drawing near,
Each moment's a step in a whimsical show,
With laughter flowing like a brook's flow.

Coffee spills are a painter's dream,
In spills and thrills, we often beam,
Every mishap adds to the score,
Crafting a life we all adore.

So cherish the quirks and the fun in store,
Life's melody rings from ceiling to floor,
With laughter leading the silly way,
In the grand show of each bright day.

**Euphoria Wrapped in Morning's Arms**

Early rays tickle my nose,
Coffee bubbles, the aroma flows.
Socks mismatched, I'm dressed in glee,
Morning wonders, come laugh with me.

Birds in mismatched serenades,
Chasing dreams in leafy glades.
A squirrel steals my last croissant,
He grins wide, "I'm the breakfast savant!"

Chasing clouds, we dance with glee,
Sunshine whispers secrets to me.
Laughter bounces from tree to tree,
What a joyful sight to see!

With pancakes stacked as high as peaks,
We giggle 'til our laughter leaks.
Wrapped in warmth, this day has spun,
In the arms of laughter, we are one.

## A Stroll Through the Garden of Hours

In the garden where time unfolds,
Frogs wear crowns; their tales are bold.
Bees buzz in a comedic waltz,
While flowers giggle, and tulips halt.

A snail slips on a leaf so bright,
"Race you to the end!"—what a sight!
Time tiptoes past, with a silly grin,
Laughing at where the day's been.

We find humor in every bug,
Sipping dew from a morning mug.
Petals whisper jokes on the wind,
In this garden, giggles never end.

Twirl and prance through the vibrant hue,
Each moment brings laughter anew.
Mirth blooms thick, it's no charade,
In this garden, merriment is made.

## **Glistening Petals of Time**

Raindrops dance upon grass blades,
Laughter echoes as humor cascades.
A flower sneezes, petals aflutter,
"Oops! Excuse me!" it starts to stutter.

Time ticks slowly as we recline,
Giggling at ants in a funny line.
Butterflies wear dapper suits, so neat,
"Who wore it best?" We can't take the heat!

Roses blush with a wink or two,
Their secrets tickle just like the dew.
Every petal a joke, delicately placed,
In this garden, we're humorously graced.

From shadows long to sunlight bright,
Every moment wraps the day in light.
In gleeful petals, joy entwined,
With laughs and giggles, it's perfectly designed.

## **Poetry Woven in the Fabric of Light**

Words of laughter weave through the air,
Jokes bounce high without a care.
Light tickles the notes we play,
Creating humor in the light of day.

Rhymes with wiggles and jigs abound,
Chasing giggles around the town.
Each syllable shines like a beam,
In this playful, whimsical dream.

Banter dances in the golden rays,
Crafting snippets of funny displays.
As shadows chuckle and sunbeams sway,
Poetry sprinkles laughter our way.

When the clock ticks its final chime,
We'll laugh with words that dance in time.
In every line, joy takes its flight,
Woven in moments, so sunny and bright.

## **Radiant Echoes**

Sunlight spills with a giggle,
Birds dance like they're on the move,
Grass tickles toes of the sprightly,
Ants parade in their busy groove.

Clouds wear hats made of cotton,
Butterflies flutter in dismay,
Bees buzz by with a gossip,
Wonder what they're up to today.

Colors burst like a jester's laugh,
Smiles bloom on the faces around,
Laughter bubbles from the brook,
Nature's jesters make silly sound.

Even the trees sway in jest,
Leaves tickle the air with a tease,
The sun slides down with a wink,
Night's blanket drapes with a squeeze.

## The Laughter in the Breeze

A breeze whispers jokes to the flowers,
Tickling petals like old best friends,
With each gust, the daisies chuckle,
As if the world just never ends.

Squirrels chase their imaginary tails,
While the sun plays peek-a-boo games,
Shadows stretch with a playful grin,
While laughter dances like flame.

The sky cracks jokes with the clouds,
Someone gets pranked with a raindrop,
All around, the day is a giggle,
Where even the wrinkles can hop.

Time slips by in silly fashion,
Watches spin like a top gone mad,
Every moment, a punchline lands,
And in the chaos, we've all had.

## Soft Murmurs of Dawn

Morning yawns with a smirk,
Stretching light across the hill,
Birds tune their morning chorus,
With notes that make the heart thrill.

Coffee swirls like a playful dance,
Steam rises in a cheeky way,
Caffeine smiles at sleepy heads,
Waking dreams must sip and sway.

Frogs croak jokes from the pond's edge,
With tadpoles laughing in the light,
Every creature joins the fun,
As shadows vanish from the night.

A sunbeam slips through the window,
Catching dust motes in a race,
The dawn giggles softly now,
As day unfolds with a warm embrace.

## **Vibrant Threads of Daybreak**

Crayons spill from the sky today,
Coloring streets with hues so bright,
Children chase their shadows around,
Playing tag with the morning light.

Bicycles zoom with silly sounds,
Wheels chirp like a comedic band,
Faces shine with delight and joy,
As laughter spreads across the land.

Kites soar high in a playful game,
Whipping tails in the cheerful air,
While clouds drift by with smirks, it seems,
Whispering secrets without a care.

Sunsets paint the sky like jesters,
With reds and purples on display,
Nighttime giggles, a luscious laugh,
As stars begin to light the way.

**Captured in the Ordinary**

A squirrel stole my sandwich,
Chasing crumbs with glee,
In the park, I watched him dance,
A lunch thief, carefree.

Children giggled wildly,
Chasing shadows by the trees,
Wondering where time goes,
In the soft, cool breeze.

The coffee shop was buzzing,
With laughter and sweet smells,
An old man told wild stories,
Of fish that winked and fell.

Every moment holds magic,
Just open up your eyes,
In the simplest of places,
Laughter often lies.

**Spinning Tales in Fleeting Time**

A bee buzzed 'round my donut,
He found it quite divine,
I waved him off politely,
But he swore he'd wait in line!

The clock ticked with annoyance,
As socks mismatched their pairs,
I grinned, my feet looked silly,
Laughter danced through the air.

Birds were crooning sweet-notes,
In a tree of vibrant green,
They whispered all the secrets,
Of the fun we'd yet to glean.

Each tick and tock a story,
Each laugh a little rhyme,
The ordinary dazzles,
In this fleeting stroll of time.

## Delights of a Sunbeam

Sunshine spills like honey,
On the pavement, warm and bright,
I tripped upon a puddle,
And landed out of sight!

A cat with an attitude,
Sat basking in the rays,
He squinted at my laughter,
Like I was gone astray.

A frisbee flew like an eagle,
And landed in a tree,
The dog just shrugged and snoozed,
Claiming it wasn't free.

Every ray brings a giggle,
To the day's simple plan,
We dance with silly shadows,
A sunbeam-loving clan.

## Petals on the Path

Petals drift from blossoms,
Like confetti in the air,
I caught one on my nose,
And then I struck a glare!

Dandelions hold court,
With their crown of sunny gold,
"Make a wish!" they whisper,
As if secrets they behold.

A puppy chased the breeze,
Rolling head over heels,
While I laughed at his antics,
And tasted jelly meals.

In every step, a giggle,
In every glance, delight,
The day's a simple treasure,
With laughter shining bright.

## The Canvas of Routine

Wake up, stretch, then spill my tea,
Cat on the counter, it's a sight to see.
Shoes mismatched, socks in a whirl,
Life's a painting, watch it twirl!

Breakfast burnt, it's a daily feat,
Trying to juggle toast and a tweet.
Mirror grins back, hair like a bird,
Laughter erupts without a word.

Chasing tasks like a game of tag,
Dodging laundry, oh what a drag!
But in this chaos, joy we'll find,
Routine's a canvas, wonderfully blind.

In the midst of all this fun,
Life's routine can feel like a pun.
With every quirk, every little surprise,
Let's laugh along 'til we're wise!

## Essence of a Sunday Stroll

Sundays come with a timid grace,
Coffee spills on my sleepy face.
Socks still damp from last week's wash,
Yet, off I go, with a merry quash.

Strolling slow through the park's old charm,
Squirrels plotting some secret alarm.
I trip on a twig, make a scene,
Hare's giggling; oh, to be keen!

Ice cream melting down my hand,
A sticky fate I had not planned.
But laughter bubbles, oh what a treat,
Every fumble makes my day complete.

With every footstep, and every cheer,
Life's essence sparkles; it's crystal clear.
In every mundane, there's silly delight,
As Sunday strolls fade into the night!

## **Glimmers of Joy in Motion**

Dancing down the street like it's a show,
Sidewalk cracks become rhythm, you know?
Sweaters mismatched in daring array,
Strutting my stuff in a quirky ballet.

Wobbling on bikes, trying to steer,
A squirrel just stole my lunch, oh dear!
Laughter erupts when I tumble and sway,
Spontaneous joy in the light of day.

Every kindly stranger, a wink or a smile,
Turns the ordinary into worthwhile.
In the dance of life, let's keep it light,
With giggles and wiggles, we'll take flight!

Glancing at clouds, their shapes so bold,
Imagination soars as stories unfold.
In life's gentle chaos, a truth we find,
It's the glimmers that spark in the playful mind!

## Serene Awakenings

Mornings greet with a sleepy sigh,
Sunlight's a tickle, oh my, oh my!
Yawning cats on windowsills,
Dreams linger on in cozy spills.

Coffee brews with a gurgling tune,
Clumsy steps dance like a cartoon.
Socks on the wrong feet, oh what a sight,
Bringing the day with pure delight.

Each moment a chuckle, each giggle a prize,
Chasing toast like it's on the rise.
The world outside shimmers in glee,
A serenade of bliss, wait and see!

In stillness found on a gentle morn,
A misstep leads to laughter reborn.
In these calm awakenings, we truly play,
Happiness bubbles; it's a whimsical way!

**Tides of Joy in a Timeless Flow**

Waves of laughter crash ashore,
Tickling toes and wanting more.
Seagulls squawk in silly flight,
Chasing dreams in broad daylight.

Buckets spill as sandcastles fade,
Bright umbrellas dance in parade.
Children's giggles echo clear,
Whispers of sunshine drawing near.

Ice cream drips on sticky hands,
While we shall feast on snack-time plans.
Footprints left as time does wane,
Memories like waves, always remain.

In this playful, sunny scene,
Life's a circus, bright and keen.
Unicorns with silly hats,
Ridding worries, chasing cats.

## Flickers of Light in the Heart

Bubbles rise with hearty cheer,
Wobbling hopes that dance so near.
Every giggle ignites a spark,
Lighting pathways through the dark.

Sunbeams tickle, chase the shade,
Puppies prance in a joyous parade.
Candles sputter, cakes go plop,
Life's a party, never stop!

In our pockets, wishes dwell,
Jokes exchanged, we cast a spell.
Tickled pink with every jest,
In this game, we are all blessed.

Days unfold like ninja fights,
Kites soar high, reaching new heights.
With each laugh, a note we write,
In the album of pure delight.

## A Symphony of Colors in Bloom

Painted skies in vibrant hues,
Splashes of laughter, playful blues.
Flowers giggle, petals sway,
Nature sings in a funny way.

Dancing leaves with cheeky flair,
Wind whispers secrets through the air.
Bouncy bunnies hop about,
While the sun just peeks to shout.

The rainbow's bow is quite the tease,
Tickling noses with mischievous breeze.
In every nook, a burst unfolds,
A treasure trove of fun it holds.

Laughter erupts like a spring rain,
In this chaos, joy's our gain.
Colors blend in wild display,
A canvas brightens each new day.

## Chronicles of Bliss Under the Sun

Sunscreen battles with the sun,
Splashing water, the ultimate fun.
Sandy shoes and messy hair,
Smile wide, without a care.

Picnics packed with treats galore,
Sandwiches play hide-and-seek in store.
Limes in drinks, a twist of fate,
Every sip feels oh-so-great.

Tales of clowns on summer's stage,
Juggling life at every age.
Barbecues with sizzling flair,
Dancing flames melt every care.

Friends unite 'neath golden rays,
Sharing stories of their days.
Underneath this endless sun,
We find the jest, we find the fun.

## **Kaleidoscope of Daytime Delights**

Sunrise giggles, colors bright,
Dancing shadows, quite a sight.
Coffee spills on pancake piles,
Laughter echoes, sunny smiles.

Bees in bowties, buzzing cheer,
Squirrels in suits, drawing near.
Jellybean skies, candy floss,
Who knew days could have such gloss?

Frisbees fly like boomerangs,
While dogs chase tails and little prangs.
Sidewalks filled with silly walks,
Sunshine plays while nature talks.

Endless moments, playful glee,
Riddles from a bumblebee.
Every hour brings a jest,
Life, it seems, is at its best.

## The Song of Rustling Trees

Trees tell secrets in the breeze,
With silly whispers through the leaves.
A gnarled trunk, a dancing grin,
Nature's laughter, where to begin?

Chipmunks audition for a play,
Starring acorns, bright and gay.
Branches sway, a merry jig,
Even the chipper ants are big.

Breezes chuckle, tickle bugs,
While squirrels trade their shiny jugs.
The sun winks down as if to say,
"Let's make mischief, come what may!"

Together they sing a clumsy tune,
Bouncing under a cartoon moon.
Rustling fun, a leafy spree,
Join the dance of the wise old tree!

## Basking in the Warmth of Today

The sun is playing peek-a-boo,
With fluffy clouds, a perfect view.
Pigeons strut in stylish sync,
While kids plot ways to throw a wink.

Lemonade stands on every street,
Chasing ice cream drips with feet.
Every corner holds a treat,
Candy wrappers dance and greet.

Picnics with ants in a line,
While squirrels crash the party fine.
Jokes unfold, the laughter rolls,
Big dreams filled with silly goals.

Oh the joy, it fills the air,
A rainbow captured in a chair.
Mirthful memories on display,
Here's to the fun of every day!

## Fragments of Time in Sunbeams

Sunbeams tickle, racing mid-air,
Shadows play hide and seek with care.
Fragments of laughter, bright and bold,
Little moments, worth more than gold.

Kites soar high, painting the sky,
While giggles escape, oh so spry.
Time hiccups, a funny tune,
Silly moments that make hearts swoon.

Butterflies wiggle in a spree,
Chasing sunspots, wild and free.
Every second, a joyful leap,
As daylight whispers, "Don't you sleep!"

In the dance of time, we play,
Collecting smiles throughout the day.
Dreams drench us in a warm embrace,
As sunbeams paint the world with grace.

## Radiant Journeys Through Light

In morning's glow, a cat may prance,
Chasing sunbeams with a silly dance.
A shoe's a castle, a hat's a crown,
In this bright world, we never frown.

Butterflies giggle, the clouds play peek,
Tugging at strings of a kite gone weak.
Laughter spills like a joyful stream,
As squirrels plot their nutty dream.

A sandwich sings with a pickle's cheer,
While ants form lines for a feast right here.
Under blue skies, our worries take flight,
Every silly moment feels so right.

As daylight fades, we twirl and sway,
Chasing shadows that dance and play.
With friends beside, the stars ignite,
In every giggle, the world feels light.

## Grace in Each Gentle Gesture

A toddler trips with a candy grin,
Spilling skeptically sweet, on a whim.
Each movement's a dance, however clumsy,
In giggles of joy, we all feel fuzzy.

A bird sings loudly, not a care to share,
While pigeons strut like they own the air.
With grace and flair, they wobble and hop,
Who knew that elegance had a flip-flop?

The breeze whispers secrets to the trees,
Leaves do the cha-cha, in sync with ease.
Every sway tells a tale of delight,
As laughter pops like a fizzy sprite.

Under the sun, we twirl and cheer,
Life's little moments are all we endear.
With playful hearts, we dance in the glow,
Creating our stories as we joyfully flow.

## A Whisper of Loneliness, a Shade of Joy

A sock says goodnight to its partner lost,
With quiet whispers, it counts the cost.
A lonely shoe thinks it's quite a clown,
Hoping for feet to bring it around.

Clouds drift lazily, with moody sighs,
While flowers laugh at their gloomy ties.
But here comes the sun with a wink and grin,
Chasing those blues with a cheerful spin.

Each cautious step can feel like a game,
Twisting and turning, we stake our claim.
In shadows we find a giggle or two,
With whispers of hope peeking through.

So toast to the day when the world feels gray,
And find a bright laugh along the way.
For joy dances lightly where loners may tread,
In every soft whisper, laughter can spread.

## **Savoring Every Moment in Time**

Tick tock goes the clock, a funny chime,
It laughs at our rush, all in a rhyme.
Jellybeans dance on the kitchen floor,
While spoons and forks argue, "Who's the lore?"

Muffins chime in with a sugary glee,
Telling the tales of sweet ecstasy.
With each little bite, we giggle and sigh,
As crumbs tumble down, oh my, oh my!

In the leap of a frog, or splash of a wave,
Life's silly moments we always crave.
With smiles in our pockets, we'll cherish time,
In a world full of whimsy, we think it's prime.

So let's sip our tea with a dash of laugh,
Embracing each moment, we'll take a photograph.
For joy's little bursts in the routine of the day,
Are the treasures we gather along the way.

## Caress of a Soft Afternoon

Sunbeams play hide and seek,
Chasing shadows near my feet.
A picnic of giggles unfolds,
As time drips like honey, sweet.

Grass tickles my toes just so,
While ants hold a surprise show.
I watch them march, a silly parade,
Planning a feast with crumbs they tow.

Butterflies tease my wandering eyes,
Donning costumes in a grand disguise.
Each flutter, a secret joke,
While I nibble on soft baked pies.

In this playful, sunlit game,
Every smile shouts my name.
Time doesn't hurry, it just won't care,
In this soft afternoon, nothing is the same.

## Voices of the Wandering Clouds

Clouds drift by, a fluffy crew,
Mimicking shapes, just for you.
One's a puppy, one's a hat,
They giggle and tease, oh how they do!

They share stories of laughter sky-high,
While raindrops perform a comic fly-by.
Chasing rainbows on a whim,
The sunlight winks, oh me, oh my!

Jokes float softly on gentle breeze,
While shadows dance with willful ease.
I'll catch a joke with my outstretched hand,
Whispering secrets through leafy trees.

A parade of silliness, clouds collide,
Creating a funny atmosphere wide.
In the sky's light-hearted comedy,
They play with dreams that they provide.

## Symphony of Laughter in the Air

Birds compose a jazzful tune,
Squirrels drum under the moon.
The breeze whispers, soft and bright,
As laughter bursts like a balloon.

Children giggle, chasing the sun,
In a world where whimsy's just begun.
Their joy dances down the lane,
Inviting each passerby for fun.

Leaves rustle, a comedic cheer,
Nature conducts, so loud and clear.
Peeking through, a joyful parade,
With each muffled laugh, it draws near.

In a symphonic, breezy affair,
The air is thick with giggles to share.
Every moment, a playful cheer,
In this laughter-filled, happy layer.

## **Dreams Carried on the Winds**

Winds whisper stories from afar,
Of waddling ducks and dancing stars.
Kites dip and dive, a silly flight,
Bringing tales where laughter jars.

Each gust carries a playful scheme,
A tickle here, a silly dream.
I chase the clouds with a hearty laugh,
In a world where things aren't what they seem.

The breeze jiggles my hat askew,
As I wander in adventures new.
With every breeze, a chuckle shared,
Days are brighter, laughs renew!

So let the winds spin tales of fun,
With dizzying twists, we're never done.
In this world of merry play,
We'll keep on dancing 'til we see the sun.

## Tapestry of Twilight

As the sun droops low in the sky,
I witness a squirrel wearing a tie.
He flips on his shades, looks quite the sight,
Chasing loose acorns, oh what a fright!

Birds hold a meeting on the old fence post,
Arguing loudly, whom they like most.
The cat on the prowl sneezes with glee,
A ruckus erupts, oh what fun to see!

A breeze tosses leaves like confetti in air,
A duck waddles by, pretending to care.
With each little quack, he's the life of the show,
Making the sunset chuckle, don't you know?

In twilight's embrace, laughter does peep,
As shadows dance lightly, they leap and they creep.
The final bow comes with a wink and a cheer,
Even the moon giggles, 'till I disappear!

## Unveiling the Ordinary

Morning yawns wide, what a silly sight,
Coffee spills over, oh what a fright!
The toaster decides it's not in the mood,
Burnt toast for breakfast, I'm very ill-sued!

The cat leaps like a pro, but misses the chair,
Lands in the laundry, fur everywhere!
Watching the curtains dance with some flair,
As if they know secrets, caught unaware.

Dogs bark their gossip, squirrels plot schemes,
While the neighbors toss in their sleeping dreams.
Each sound's a reminder, life's merriest play,
In the grand, elegant mess of the day.

With giggles from children, joy races past,
In this jumbled carnival, unsurpassed.
Who knew the mundane had such a knack,
To bring forth the smiles, never hold back!

**Nature's Quiet Adoration**

Morning dew glistens like tiny glass beads,
A worm waxes poetic, reciting his needs.
With every soft wiggle, he gives it a whirl,
While flowers nod gently, putting on a twirl.

Bumblebees buzz like they're DJing a beat,
Dandelions dance with nimble little feet.
Even the rocks have a tale to tell,
As ants march along, saying all is well!

Oh, ducks in a pond, with synchronized flair,
Quacking their anthem, light as air.
Nature's a stage where hilarity thrives,
A comedy sketch where each creature dives!

As evening folds in, with giggles in tow,
Fireflies flicker, putting on a show.
Underneath the laughter, the world finds its grace,
In each funny moment, a delightful embrace!

## **Starlit Reflections**

The sun waves goodbye with a cheeky grin,
As stars burst forth, laughter begins.
Moon tricks the sleepies, 'You're not done yet,'
With dreams on the line, a fun little bet.

Clouds play hopscotch, leaping so light,
Casting shadows that tickle the night.
A comet zooms past, yelling, "Whoa, what fun!"
While the world giggles, 'Oh, aren't we all one?'

The night holds secrets wrapped in delight,
Jokes from the galaxies, taking their flight.
With twinkling eyes, they share in our play,
Reflecting the humor of an earthly ballet.

As bedtime approaches, the laughter draws near,
With whispers of nonsense, and calmness, my dear.
So dream with a chuckle, let worries take wing,
In the vastness of night, oh, what joy to bring!

## Reflections in a Pool of Joy

In a puddle, a frog does prance,
Wearing a crown, it dares to dance.
Splashing water, the dog barks loud,
Echoing laughter, oh, so proud!

A turtle swims by, all in a haze,
Wondering why, we're in such a craze.
It flips on its back, what a sight,
Telling the sun, it's ready to bite!

The clouds giggle, cover the sun,
While the kids on the swings just run.
Falling down with a squeaky shriek,
Rolling around, oh, how they squeak!

But as the sun sets, it's time to go,
With pockets full of laughter, in long shadows.
Frogs and turtles, take a bow,
Tomorrow's puddles, we'll leap! But how?

## Hues of Wonder in the Sky

Oh, the clouds wear hats that float,
While I wave from my little boat.
The sun's a chef, grilling rays,
While moonwalkers dance in daze.

Rainbows slide down from up high,
Sliding down with a joyful sigh.
Little birds tweet in perfect rhyme,
Claiming they're the stars of this time!

Bubbles burst with a squeaky pop,
As children chase them, hop and hop.
The wind throws whispers, all playful tunes,
Dancing along with bright afternoon moons.

As the colors blend and swirl,
Each hue a giggle, each bend a whirl.
What fun these painted skies can give,
In this vibrant world, we love to live!

**Flavors of Life in a Glass**

Lemonade's sweet, gives a zesty cheer,
While pickles swim, oh dear, oh dear!
Ice cubes clink like a band on stage,
Every sip, a new flavor gauge.

Cola giggles, tickles your nose,
While soda dances, it surely knows.
Strawberries leap with a fruity splash,
They taste the rainbow in a big glass crash!

Mango twirls, a smooth ballet,
As cherries giggle, 'please, let us stay!'
Bottoms up, let's down this brew,
Smile wide, for the fun's just for you!

As the glass empties, laughter remains,
With sticky fingers, and silly refrains.
Let's mix it up for another round,
In this tasty world, joy can be found!

## Passages of Time in Childlike Play

Tick-tocks giggle as minutes flee,
While kids play games, oh let them be!
Jumping in puddles, splish-splash loud,
Each droplet bursts like laughter's crowd.

Sandcastles rise to the calling tide,
While seagulls swoop and glide beside.
Every grain tells a silly tale,
Of knights and dragons, of happy trails!

Glow-in-the-dark stars begin to twinkle,
As bedtime approaches, oh, how they crinkle.
But stories whisk them far away,
In dreams where they dance, and often sway.

With morning light, they leap and run,
Smiling at shadows, chasing the sun.
A carousel of joy, round and round,
In the heart of play, happiness is found!

## Joy in the Heart of Springtime

In spring's bright bloom, the frogs wear hats,
Dancing 'round the garden, like chubby cats.
The flowers gossip about the bees,
While giggling daisies sway in the breeze.

Birds build nests with bits of twine,
They argue over who gets the best vine.
A squirrel juggles acorns with flair,
As the sun winks and plays on a dare.

Little children chase after the kite,
Who runs away at a comical height.
While puddles reflect their laughter loud,
Sprinkling joy like a playful cloud.

With butterflies twirling, making a show,
Each one's a dancer, putting on a glow.
In the heart of spring, laughter's our thing,
The world skips along, like a happy fling.

## Enchantment in Every Hour

In the morning light, toast starts to sing,
Jam makes a joke, oh what a zing!
Cereal bounces, a whimsical dance,
While coffee snores, not taking a chance.

Time tickles clocks that have lost their way,
Each second giggles, 'Let's make it play!'
The sun paints smiles on curious faces,
While socks have arguments in strange places.

At noon, the shadows perform a charade,
As lunchbox treasures seem quite delayed.
Sandwiches chat while pickles just pout,
Then glance at the chips for a good shout-out.

As the day fades, stars start to prance,
While the moon dresses up for a nightly dance.
Every hour's filled with laughter galore,
In this whimsical world, who could ask for more?

## Tapestry of Golden Moments

Time unravels like a silly string,
Weave together laughs, let the good times fling.
A kitten sneezes, it's quite the display,
As yarn balls roll in a mischievous fray.

Picnics abound with sandwiches that talk,
They whisper secrets while ants take a walk.
Balloons float by with giggles galore,
As friends share stories and laughter, what's more?

Golden moments shimmer like stars up high,
As the clouds make faces, drifting on by.
The sun throws confetti, what a grand affair,
With shadows now giggling, light as a flare.

The evening brings tales of silly delight,
While fireflies shine in the soft twilight.
Each twinkle a spark that brightens our night,
In this tapestry woven, everything feels right.

## Serenity in Shades of Twilight

As twilight falls, the crickets begin,
With a serenade soft, a whimsical spin.
Fireflies flicker, like winks from the past,
In the hush of the night, the fun isn't fast.

Cats hold court on the fence, having debates,
About the best way to catch little mates.
With a sigh from the stars, they settle the score,
As night wraps the world in its velvety lore.

Mice dance under the moon's gentle gaze,
While owls chuckle, lost in a haze.
Nostalgic and funny, the night takes its claim,
Every shadow's a character in this mystical game.

And laughter echoes in the stillness so deep,
Reminding us all to embrace and to keep,
The serenity wrapped in hues soft and bright,
In shades of the twilight, laughter takes flight.

## Chapters Written in Sunlit Shadows

In a world where socks can dance,
The sunbeams join the silly prance.
A cat wears shades, quite out of style,
While squirrels plot to steal a smile.

The dog in shades thinks he's a star,
As birds critique his fashion bar.
A lollipop gets dropped and rolled,
While ice cream dreams of stories told.

The tree sways gently, sings a tune,
As grasshoppers launch to the moon.
A frog croaks jokes to every passer,
Making waves with each leap, oh how they'll laster!

Underneath the gleeful skies,
Laughter dances, never lies.
The world is wacky, bright, and fun,
In shadows where the giggles run.

**The Palette of a Perfect Day**

With crayons in a crinkled case,
A rainbow soon will show its face.
The sun spills colors on the ground,
While playful thoughts spin round and round.

A jellybean rolls, it takes its stand,
Pretending it's the boss of the band.
The trees are clapping in delight,
As butterflies take flight, oh what a sight!

The clouds play tag, they chase the sun,
While ants on parade declare it fun.
The flowers giggle, tickled pink,
In gardens where the fairies wink.

With a painted sky of giggly hues,
Each moment sings, ignites our muse.
In this madness, we all sway,
A masterpiece in fun display.

## Horizons Filled with Endless Possibilities

Balloon animals float up high,
While clouds tease dreams that can't deny.
A lemonade stand starts a race,
As kids rush in to claim their space.

The ice cream man wears polka dots,
Trying to outsmart sneaky tots.
With flavors so absurdly bright,
One's confused if it's day or night.

A picnic basket starts to dance,
As ants form lines, determined stance.
A sandwich wears a tiny hat,
Declaring war on that pesky rat!

Horizons hum with all that's new,
Where everything seems to woohoo.
In this land of joyful spree,
We laugh and shout, 'Oh, let it be!'

## Secrets of the Day in Sunbeams

A cupcake whispers sweet today,
While sunlight giggles as it plays.
A daisy winks from soft green grass,
Inviting butterflies to pass.

The sunbeams hide behind a tree,
Playing peek-a-boo, wild and free.
A bear in shades reads a book,
As honeybees take a closer look.

A squirrel juggles acorns galore,
While rabbits cheer, 'We want more!'
The sky turned upside down with fun,
As laughter melts into the sun.

Secrets shared in shadows grow,
With smiles that overflow, you know.
In these moments, bright and sweet,
Life's all about the funny treat.

**Flickering Moments in the Sun**

Squirrels on a quest, chasing their tails,
While bees hold court, sipping on pails.
A rogue kite floats, just out of reach,
As laughter spills out, like salt from a peach.

Sunbeams bounce off the kids in the park,
As ice cream drips, oh what a lark!
Giggles and shrieks, the air full of glee,
While ants march on, a comical spree.

Picnic blankets wave in the breeze,
As sandwiches vanish like magic, if you please!
With every bite comes a story to share,
Creating a ruckus, without a care.

So here's to the moments, both silly and bright,
The laughter and joy, oh what a sight!
Capturing bliss in a flash of the sun,
We'll remember these days, oh how we've spun!

## The Story Written in Shadows

Shadows dancing upon the old brick walls,
As cats plot schemes and each one licks paws.
Beneath the oak, a squirrel does boast,
Of lands uncharted, or so he can post.

Footsteps tracing tales of the slips and the falls,
While puddles giggle, reflecting the calls.
A paper boat sails down the gutter,
While ducks engage in an unnecessary mutter.

The sun starts to dip, casting hues so grand,
A shadowed figure holds a jellybean band.
Before it can form, it glasses the ground,
But joy's not a shadow, it's always around.

So let's paint the paths where laughter can grow,
With tales of mischief, let silliness flow!
For every shadow, a grin's ultimate trick,
In this whimsical world, life's joys come quick.

## **Lullabies of Lost Hours**

Whispers of time, in the tick of a clock,
While frogs croak tunes from the edge of the dock.
Children run wild, questions in tow,
As clouds become sheep, ready to flow.

Swing sets creak with tales from above,
Where daydreams stir and giggles push shoves.
Cupcakes and cookies line up in a row,
While sprinkles dance, just putting on a show.

The sun starts to yawn, a goodbye so sweet,
As stars take their turn, the evening's treat.
With fireflies blinking, like winking friends,
The lullabies play, the laughter never ends.

So gather the moments, in jars oh so bright,
Seal them with giggles, a bundle of light.
Savor the hours, don't let them escape,
For life's a grand tale, a magical shape.

## **Radiance in Every Step**

Each footfall sparks, like fireworks in June,
As puddles giggle under the afternoon moon.
Grass stains mark trails of adventures so grand,
While our hearts keep rhythm, as pulses expand.

Wobbling bikes take to the paths of the street,
With misplaced pedals and shoes on the beat.
Tiptoeing past like a cat on a prowl,
The dance of the day takes a whimsical bow.

Rainbows of laughter break barriers down,
As joy shoots through like a worn, crazy crown.
Every chuckle echoes, of joy that we sip,
Life bursts with color in every small trip.

So let's tread with wonder, embrace every phase,
With smiles and stories to brighten our gaze.
For in each little step, there lies pure delight,
An orchestra of nonsense that feels just right.

## The Happiness of a Gentle Breeze

A gentle breeze tickles my nose,
Whispers secrets that nobody knows.
It plays with my hat, a cheeky old friend,
Dancing around till I can't comprehend.

It swirls past my ears, causing me to grin,
Like a playful ghost eager to win.
I chase after it, but it's too quick to catch,
Laughing behind me, a friendly mismatch.

The trees join the fun, swaying with glee,
Making such noise, you'd think it's a spree.
Leaves are high-fiving while branches embrace,
In this lively game, I'm losing my pace.

With each gust that rolls, I can't help but smile,
Nature's own jokes, with a whimsical style.
Puddles are hopping, mud flies as I whirl,
In the breeze's charm, I twirl like a girl.

## Sunshine Drifting Through Leaves

Sunshine drips down, like honey on bread,
Tickling the branches, where squirrels have tread.
The light makes them dance, those cheeky little pests,
Waving at shadows, they're on quite the quest.

It kisses my cheeks and warms up my toes,
A brilliant spotlight on all that it glows.
I squint at the world, in this golden embrace,
While bugs in the air engage in a race.

The warmth wraps around like a blanket of cheer,
As birds start their concert, loud and quite clear.
They croon about seeds and share tales of the sky,
I chuckle to think how they've mastered the high.

With each sizzle of light, laughter spills forth,
And suddenly shadows can't hide their worth.
Sunshine drifts gently, through leaves high above,
While I'm left below, filled with warmth and love.

## Echoed Laughter in the Afternoon

In the afternoon glow, laughter rings clear,
Bouncing like tennis balls, oh what a cheer!
Kids on the swings are masters of play,
Chasing each other, come join the fray!

The dog joins the party, he's leaping for fun,
Diving for shadows, outsmarting the sun.
With barks and with giggles, they all form a crew,
What a ruckus they make, who knew it was true?

I sit with my drink, trying hard not to spill,
As bursts of pure joy create quite the thrill.
A banana peel slips, and oh, here comes the fall,
Their squeals turn to chuckles, it's a wonderful ball!

Sun-kissed shenanigans unfold before me,
As laughter echoes, wild and free.
In this midst of delight, it's hard to stay gray,
For laughter and sunshine will brighten my day.

## A Symphony of Everyday Wonders

Everyday moments create quite the show,
Bees buzzing loudly, putting on a glow.
A dog in the grass is a true maestro,
Chasing its tail, like a spitfire, whoa!

The kettle whistles, a high-pitched delight,
As spoons start to dance, in mid-air flight.
The toast pops up, and I jump in my chair,
Caught in the rhythm, I join with a flair.

Flip-flops parade on a path made of sun,
While clouds play the keys, with a wink and some fun.
Footsteps create a beat on this lively street,
Every corner I turn, another joy I meet.

A symphony rises from the simplest things,
From laughter of children to chirping that rings.
In mundane moments, surprises abound,
Nature's sweet orchestra, forever unbound.

## A Canvas of Fleeting Whispers

Birds in pajamas flap around,
Sipping coffee without a sound.
Cats wear hats, they strut with pride,
As squirrels dance, the trees their guide.

Sunshine peeks through curtains drawn,
While toast pops up, a crispy yawn.
Sock puppets debate on who's the best,
Bringing giggles to a lazy nest.

Time ticks by in a funny way,
Mice hold talks about the play.
Each second winks, so full of cheer,
As laughter echoes, far and near.

In puddles, frogs wear tiny shoes,
While ants take bets, they cannot lose.
With every tick, a funny tale,
The world spins on, without fail.

## Melodies of Ordinary Miracles

Raindrops tap on the window pane,
Pigeons gossip, they're quite insane.
A dog sings opera out of tune,
While crickets hum a jazzy rune.

Bubbles rise from a soapy pot,
As dad declares he's lost the plot.
Bananas slip with style and grace,
Chasing balls in a silly race.

Mailboxes wear a goofy frown,
While neighborhood kids all gather round.
The ice cream truck is blaring loud,
And dancing solos, the pets are proud.

Clouds giggle as they drift and sway,
Bringing shadows to dance and play.
Every moment's a silly spree,
With random joys, so wild and free.

## Dancing Shadows in the Glow

Moonbeams waltz on the garden grass,
While wind chimes rattle, sighing alas.
Fireflies twirl in a joyous flight,
Making wishes beneath the night.

Stars giggle as they blink and shine,
As cats play chess, sipping on wine.
The trees can't stop their freestyle moves,
Grooving gently in playful grooves.

Jellybeans roll on the sidewalk wide,
While puddles hold a giggly tide.
Each shadow leaps, a fleeting sight,
In swirling patterns of sheer delight.

Time does cartwheels, full of cheer,
As clocks wear glasses, can't see near.
Every tick brings a new dance trend,
In this wacky world, around the bend.

## **Luminous Threads of Everyday Life**

A toast to mornings in mismatched socks,
Where coffee spills in joyful shocks.
Muffins giggle as they bake,
And eggs make jokes for laughter's sake.

Sunscreen fights with wandering hands,
As sandcastles get built on whims and plans.
Kids wearing capes race down the lane,
While lemonade has a silly stain.

Kites that tumble and take a dive,
As laughter echoes, we feel alive.
Puppies tumble in fields of grass,
Each moment captured, it's a sweet pass.

In laughter's glow, we find our thread,
In this theater of fun, we tread.
Every tick is an offbeat rhyme,
In this zany world, it's our prime time.

www.ingramcontent.com/pod-product-compliance
Lightning Source LLC
Chambersburg PA
CBHW062112280426
43661CB00086B/495